SECRETS

SECRETS

JOSEPH JOHN THOMAS

iUniverse, Inc.
Bloomington

SECRETS

iUniverse books may be ordered through booksellers or by contacting:

iUniverse
1663 Liberty Drive
Bloomington, IN 47403
www.iuniverse.com
1-800-Authors (1-800-288-4677)

ISBN: 978-1-4620-6198-3 (sc)
ISBN: 978-1-4620-6197-6 (ebk)

Printed in the United States of America

iUniverse rev. date: 10/20/2011

Chapter 1 – My life as a child to an adult

My life as a non- Christian was very strange because I was trying to cope with an illness at a very young age. As a young infant I was cared by mother that also was recovering from illness. My mother will always have a big part in my life. As I grew out of my terrible twos and into my childhood, I became much undisciplined and somewhat a very hyper child. Living with my mother I had a bad habit with matches and one day I burnt the front of my house down. Because of my mother having trouble of taking care of my brothers, I spent most of my childhood with my aunts and uncles. My life was very strange as I grew up as a child overcoming obstacles with my hyperactivity. I was the type of kid that always had a smile on my face. Negativity and dislike was not a part of me as I was growing up. One summer I was at a new foster family and they decided to put me in a camp for a month. It wasn't just an ordinary camp it was a camp that changed my life forever! It was called Camp Pennile for Jesus. This is ware just a few verses of the bible had an emotional impact on me. It was a warm moist morning of my first day at camp as I walked out of my dorm I herd birds chirping and a group of choir singing as if they were angels. As I was standing outside of my dorm I herd a person playing a loud instrument. It sounded like an echo of deep bull frog. That day was full of games and singing gospel from the bible late that night. The days at camp went quickly because I was making friends and helping people out with there problems with their faith with Jesus Christ and God. I realized wasn't allowing my illness stop me from having a good time at camp. It was Sunday and it was time to worship, it was a time that I would never forget. They called people up by the front of the pews where the preacher was standing. He was saying if anyone doesn't have a personal relationship with God, "come to the front of the pew and come and get saved!" I knew Jesus a little bit but I wanted to know him more, so I stood up as my heart beating like a flap of a humming birds wings. I tried to keep my composure together and I walked up by the preacher and he put his hands on my head and he told me do you accept Jesus Christ died for your sins and rose from the dead and do you accept him in your heart I said yes, yes I do with tear s running down from my face that I made a relation with the son of God Jesus Christ. The month went quick as I filled my heart with the Lord my savior and warmth feeling of our creator the Lord God Almighty. That night after returning back to my foster family was coming down with being very sick in my mind with my illness unknown to doctors for that night anyways. I walked my dog outside and I looked up at the sunset and the delusions fell in thinking bazaar thoughts. That night had problem sleeping and hearing voices in my head. I was getting in an argument with my foster mom. She called the ambulance and I went impatient. In the hospital I was very sick saying that some one is going to come and get me and being paranoid. My first day in the hospital was with a breakfast and saw a group of young people. After the breakfast I went to see the doctor and he told me that I have by-pollard, ADHD, and shychitsophactive symptoms of shyctsophrania. I just looked at him and told him what is that, and he said that you have multi illnesses. The doctor told me that I have a medication for you and he said resperadal. I said what is that and he told me it will help you with your illness. It's been two days after taking the resperidal I felt the normal side effect which are fainting spells and dizziness. That day I went home and back to school.

Chapter 2- My Road to Recovery

I look back at all the hospitalizations, when I was being put on multiple medications that had so many negative side effects and I stop and think with the positive effects the medication that helps me with my illness. Feeling better on the medication allows me to cope with the illnesses that I have. I am at my best when I'm taking my medication and when I go see the doctor sometimes he adjusts the medication or sometimes even gives me a whole different kind of medication. Sometimes when the medication doesn't work and I start to get ill and then I look forward to see the doctor or even get a quick visit to the hospital to see if I need to go Impatient. Recovery is baby steps to finally get back to your feet. Everybody should have goals and dreams to obtain and look forward to in there everyday life. I have discovered I'm a very optimistic person even though sometimes I can be happy one moment and a mix of emotions the next but I'm easy to get along with when you get to know me. Being happy and positive helps me release tension and benefits me in becoming a strong willed person. My smile reveals my good sense of humor. Smiling makes you feel good about yourself and the person smiles back at you makes them feel good as person also to. I have challenged my-self to see how far I can get in becoming the greatest person I can be. A day-to- day routine of taking my medication has helped me achieve in a matter of time to become a better and healthier person among my peer and the community. I used to live in the lodge. A lodge is where people go that are almost homeless and don't have enough money to get there own place and that has to stay active in either or volunteering, working, or some kind of school work. I have found a way to higher my self esteem by self encouraging my-self in the morning and exercising during the day to live a healthier life. It's a long road to get in a better shape. My medication is helpful to me, but one of the side effects of my medication is gaining weight. Last year when I was over weight, I was doing everything to loose weight, lifting weights, riding on bikes and playing basketball. I was even on a protein diet to get some more muscles and trying to eat the right foods to stay in shape. Good hygiene is helpful and it allows me to guide my-self to a healthier and cleaner life style. Its an every day process and everybody needs to in order to stay healthy to have a good hygiene routine. I like to smell fresh and clean as in a joking manner I want to be a girl magnet to me that would be electrifying. As exercising helps me to lower my symptoms of my medication and it adjust my way of living. As I become fit, I try to encourage my friends to start exercising to. I think that I'm a positive influence to empower my peer's self-esteems in the way that I am being a positive role model towards my friends. Being in placement has helped me with structure and following rules. With getting in trouble and being disciplined helps me solve my problems and getting more mature knowing my issues and talking to either a counselor or staff, or a group of people. This helped me know deep inside that changing is not a bad thing, Changing will take time, and it's just being patient and setting a pace and taking steps. In Harbor creek I met a lot of people that had the same or close to the same problems that I had making friends is to know in that trust will always will be there, If trust is not there, than it is hard to make a friend. One gift that I have is that I can always reason to let someone know how I feel. Another placement that spent time in was keystone. I was afraid to admit my problems but as I was getting ill, I now look back to this time and remember words that I have put together to sound like this. Out of the darkness and into the light. This quote means a great deal to me because at keystone I had issues and problems, but now being better, the memory brings light back to me with a smile that can last forever. As my family encourages me to stay out of trouble and they are always there for me. In the difficult times through my hospitalizations, my brother Jake and his foster family Rose and Mark Deka always has been there for me for support. My mother who gave me life could not be there for me every day growing up, but my mom is a big part of my life and she's the best mom and tries her best as a good influence on me and my brothers. My family and close friends are my rock in my life. My family has helped me become stronger in to achieve my goals. One of my goals is working to get my G.E.D when achieving this goal has a positive outlook for me in the future. Hard work never comes easy but it always pays off in the end. I'm looking for the right momentum to keep up my studying to pass my G.E.D. Coming to Chaps is like all the staff and members are like one big friend. Taking time out of my day and volunteer and write articles for the newsletter that people read every month. Whatever I put at volunteer at Chaps comes back to me in dozen different ways in giving back to the community. Having people look and see how far I've came and knowing people in Meadville that has known me since I was little kid. Having goals and expectations is just the beginning of life. Struggling in many ways like to find your way on a dark highway. I guess you have to follow the yellow signs to lead you in the right directions. Stop and think and not let my anger control any of my actions. For me it's breath taking to figure out what I'm going to do with my life. I take ten deep breaths when I'm outside helps me to relax and relive tension. That's a tactic that has been around for decades. I've been turning my old poems into music. Particularly I have Hip-Hop on my mind, so I rap for my leisure activity. I write everyday in my journal to help me understand my feelings and emotions. I give all the energy that I have in the morning to push my-self to get my G.E.D. My mid-time goal is to go to college or in the summer after I get some money saved up. I won't to move to L.A to work on my designing career. I'm still thinking to go to college to get a business degree. For other solutions for my back problem I've learned to cope with the challenges of how to cope with a supplement called shark cartridge with helps a great deal. I do back exercises during the day and I stay loose by stretching. Having a mother and being raised up in a Catholic church was sometimes difficult. Learning the Catholic religion always kept me calm and also puzzled as a young child. I wear a crucifix cross to remember my baptism that's when you go to church on a Sunday and the preacher blesses you with Holy water. Sometimes I watch T.V instead of going to church every Sunday. Feeling doped up on medication that I take a prescription from the doctor. I have to doctors a mental health doctor and a physical health doctor. Having a back problem sets me back in keep on doing some kind of exercise during the day and learning to eat healthy also keeps my weight down. I realize it is very important to do my back exercise usually in the morning and the evening with the mixture of Yoga and Tai-chi to keep my back loose. Relaxing during the day and stretching and doing exercises are some great tactics to keep feeling healthy physically and mentally. It's very helpful when you have a problem to take supplements like shark cartilage and even a vitamin that helps me incredibly. Vitamin E boosts my energy during the day, also keeps me very healthy and allows me to have great circulation in the blood through out my whole entire body. Having pain cream for my back and taking pain killers and anti-inflammatory keeps sleepy and agile and lethargic. After reading the natural cures they don't won't you to know about, lets me know all the natural cures for the human being. Putting DMSO on my back relieve pain and inflammation at the same time. Taking pills just adds up the trouble of symptoms, when you can be symptom free! I thank Kevin Trudeau for all the natural cures. All my life I had someone there where in the need of help. I'm going to prove to everybody at Chaps that I'm going to be a successful person in living on my own. I learned everything that I needed to live by my-self. To taking advice from friends and family allows me to have skills to live in my own apartment. Writing my poetry and working on artwork allows me to filter out frustration like electricity to a circuit as being independent and living on my own builds my self-esteem and makes me feel good about my –self. Being around positive people at Chaps helps me with my problems that need to be solved. Thank you all the staff at Chaps for the guide line of my life and helping on the road to recovery. Every morning I wake –up and there's something I have to do. To making my bed in the morning, to studying for my G.E.D. homework keeps busy during the day. Starting a project for a company someday I would like to achieve one day. Working during the day that involves volunteering or working keeps me active. I've been working on my poetry for now four years. I let out my frustrations out on pen and paper to now beautiful poetry. Having high-self esteem makes me tolerable to negative words and reactions to other people that I don't know. I just let out one ear through the other ear. Having a supernatural, who I cal God helps me when I'm in need to talk to outside in the comfort of the wind. Taking my medication everyday is a struggle in my life because of the Sid effect of gaining weight.

Chapter 3 – My Relationship with God

To foster care and used to live in quality living center, you could say a little taste of Hell for me especially going through placement, but only not in spirit just in person. My brother Jake influences me in getting my G.E.D and my complete education. The only thing that scares me is death, even though I'm a Christian and being reborn as a Christian allows you to have everlasting eternal life, but my own personal belief I think everybody is afraid of something either it's a spider or if for me if it's death. Even though I'm a Christian I want my visions to become real and in the spirit through a piecing light and a paradise that God and Jesus has to come for his followers. All Christians share the relationship that has Jesus the son of God has on me and all Christians. To inherit my illness's through my family I write beautiful poetry about God and my relationship with the son and the father. I have the passion for life and now at my young adult age I'm going to keep following the footprints of Jesus and the light of God. Reading the Bible is my guideline of following the commandments and how they reflect the everyday life of laws. A kingdom awaiting for everyone to see and open there hearts to Jesus. As God told us about the Last Supper and it explains in the Bible with the Feast of Lamb. There will be a church to build with pillars and the top made from bamboo. The church will be made with golden gates. There will be also tamed animals grazing on the outside of the church, with a sight like a zoo. Included in the church will be a long table, with a feast to fill a hunger of anyone. There will be all different kinds of food that a human can think of. Everybody will be invited to the feast such as the Pope, Jews, and Christians. My second vision would be a cactus that would appear in parts of Africa, starting from a seed deep down in the earth from a seed from God. There would be fresh milk and the cactus that would bare fruit mostly the starving children in Africa. In the father I pray that this fruit cactus will appear and grow rapidly from a seed deep down in the earth in the Holy Spirit Now and forever Amen! It took me a year to match my title with this book and here it is "A Gift from God", I think that would be the perfect title for my book. I've simply narrowed my vision of once a delusion from a beanstalk now to a fruit cactus and to be as realistic as possible. My name is Joseph John Thomas and I'm a Christian. It's my visions that really appealing and hopeful to every follower of Jesus Christ. I've mentioned both of my visions to doctors and therapist all they said I am delusional but Christian and I have figured my visions are from God and they are Holy. I will adventure in to become one day a wealthy person because I would like to fund a Church that would be built for Jesus and God. I've always said you can do anything if you put your mind to it. One of my professions would be designing clothes, but first I would get my G.E.D. I'm going to turn on the switch of my brain and let it work like a light bulb. God's counting on me to make something out of this world and prepare people of the word of God and one day the returning of Jesus Christ. I think that would be awesome to be a missionary and spread the word of God and let people of all religions here about my visions. There are so many professions that are an option in this world. I've inherited my strong faith from my mother but my passion from God. Every morning I wake up and I appreciate another day In God's world. I have a gift from God that is writing all different kinds of rhyming poetry. Spending most of my time at Chaps or mental health awareness program allows me to express my-self as a good friend and to all my friends and staff here at Chaps. As knowing God as my father and his son Jesus Christ makes my as easy going to make friends in Meadville Pa. Going to bed and saying my prayers insures me with a positive relationship with the God Almighty. Writing this book has three objectives one is to have a self –help towards people that has an illness and to discover why when you have an illness to stay in touch with your psychiatrists and to lean how to cope with an illness. In my point of view I think everybody should a relationship with God and Jesus and that's the third objective. I have a strong relationship through prayer, reading the bible and excepting Jesus in my heart he knowing that he died on the cross for our sins and as did on the third day he came back from the dead to also return one day for the second coming. I walk, sing, jump, laugh, cry, eat, all those actions come from an ultimate being which is God. You can either follow the bible and ten commandments and as growing up as a child to follow rules of your parents and the laws of the government. Living with obedience and have some sort of role model in your life. In the past of having a bad day comes and goes, one day I went bowling and I was complaining of my back so I went outside and laid on the ground and started to have a conversation with God. I cleared my mind of every thing and meditated for about thirty minutes. I was praying at the same time thanking God for the trees to breathe from and the ground to be thankful to plant crops. Having God in my life changes your feelings of the relationship with yourself and God. Allowing nothing negative in my way and also ignoring the negativity that passes me during the day. Trusting and giving your whole life to put God first and put your troubles in God's hands. The consciences that are in every human, God finds in everybody to communicate through his gentle voice. Having a positive attitude where I learned from keystone, allows me to have structure in my own life living now in Meadville. At placement I saw different sides of me but now the true side of me where the light shines from my smile. I can remember one time in keystone a staff told us residents can anyone sing country music and I said," yes I can so I started sing She thinks my tractors sexy." then all the residents started to laugh. Then Mike said, "I want to se anybody else sing, The point I'm trying to get through if you have a good voice don't let any body stop you in succeeding with a career that if your voice can carry you there. One of my gifts from God is writing poetry. After I write a poem I thank God for the patience of writing poetry about the Almighty. Some of my family doesn't understand about my poetry, then I just explain to them on what each poem means to me. The analogies I use in my poems usually reflect on how I feel about the amazing God and almost all my poems is mostly about God. Most of my poems rime because I like when two words sound the same. When I wrote my poems the majority of them I wrote in 2008. It all started when I went to sit on the ground outside in the grass and asked God what I can do with my life. So the next three months I sat I my chair and wrote poem after poem. I started to put words together to form beautiful poems about God. Some of my favorites such as God go on and on, and God's the gentle voice. Thanking God everyday for fresh fruit and fresh air to breathe, plus freshwater and the sunlight to give vitamins from oils and minerals from meats. I was in the hospital when I had my first vision. My other two visions is about a fruit cactus appearing in the desert and the first supper which is mentioned in the bible as the feast of lamb. One night in the hospital I was reading a book about a circus and animals. I was sleeping and God came in my sleep as the Holy Spirit and have very large church with pillars and old vision golden paint gates It's not just going to be a ordinary church It's going to be housed of five separate long extended tables with an outside with tamed animals. The church would be called "a

Vision from God." A skylight dorm over top of the pillars and this church will contain the feast of the lamb or the first supper. I'm going into detail about my church circus will be an accesses to all living being. There will be all religions including Catholics, Jews, Christians and the believers of God. To come together to celebrate a feast, to all regions and worshiping in the name of God the father and Jesus the savior. Having goals and expectations is just the beginning stage of life. I can struggle in many ways to light up that dark highway. I guess you have to follow the yellow signs to lead you in the right directions. Taking ten deep breaths every time that I go outside is a good stress relieving tactic. When I'm frustrated at the end of the day I have a conversation with God, Is that awesome that he's everywhere.

"The three letters"

Playing football and sports can be an incentive of having fun. Allowing my illness to show in different ways, either or being humorous, laughter, and feeling a mix of emotions. As a young adult, I'm expressing many changes the chemicals in my brain as reaching the adult age. I try live a calm collective life. To the three R's restrain, refrain, and regroup. Deep breathing helps me to restrain and to refrain to stop and think before I act on my thoughts. To regroup from a issue to resolve from a problem. Adjusting, applying, and assistance of the three A's is helpful towards my multi illness's. To adjust my emotions with talk therapy and to apply exercise to your daily routine, the last A is assistance from your family, friends and staff or workers of a program to guide you on the right track. The Big C's is my most important guide line, for me being calm. collective, and to cope. To be calm is an everyday basis, to be collective with your feelings and you emotions towards your illness. Having a illness is not bad but to look for your strengths of your illness always make you feel better inside.

"Our God"

It's our God that helps us fills our goals and dreams,
It's our God that lives with our souls and spirits when we die,
It's our God that determines over killing and famine,
When we all cry even remorse over a child's little lie,
I fold my hands and pray at night, as God fills the room with his holy hands
over my head I feel without fright,
God is with us in the time of need,
It's our God that we worship and the vine of wine to sip, but not get drunk,
The love of God's creation of two Holy lights to bring life of a paradise that
will be one day insight,
It's our God to praise and thanks,
It's our God that send his son to die onthe cross for our sins and risen on the
third day,
Everyone who loves this earth wait and see and believing in his followers,
who God first believed,

By Joseph John Thomas
9-1-08

"A Church Boy"

People think I'm a dummy,
Sky cloud sunny to be happy,
Like a sore toe to a man's 1970's fro,

A give back to the poor, lottery money a year wait tell I scored,
At a personal care home, grubbing on figs, back feel like a knotted
up twig, Grubbing not wasting like, slop to a pig,

Most of all, cousin to call, breaking through glass, eye's freezing,
on the bouncing ball, mixed mutt, king earning like king Tutt,,
All churches gathering like swarming bee's, mama caring for
mass, as a kid sometimes or maybe I'll pass,

I'm a church boy, not a dummy or a toy,

Nighttime, bible reading, a vision to send, to share, why some
don't care, those puzzle stop and stare,
Ahoy brings a scent, a church forming in a tent, saving every
penny or cent,

I'm a church boy, not a dummy or a toy,

Once and still a Jesus freak, system of med's make me tweak, God
to find, signs of earth to seek, sun reveling in many way's the
mountain climber climbing pulling up every inch, for me muscle
contractions, epidermal, cinnamon like energy thermal , jumping
up on every hurtle, page turning in the Bible,

I'm a church boy, not a dummy or a toy,

By: Joseph John Thomas   2-1-08

"A Church Circus"

Church so calm, the pope is preaching, nun's be teaching,
Love to bro to sis, to remember an old women's kiss,
Smiling from cheek to cheek, to the bible I have to a peek,
Toxins entering out from s leak,

Tame to wild, loud to quite, meanwhile strong in faith,
Fish pool reeling with bait, artwork to paint,

A church circus known to me, but to all is still unknown

Masterpiece to complete, back hurts, relieves tension so take a seat, a first
supper so enjoy the feast, powder up girl, bowling fat , to a powder up yeast,

A church to see with work to build, with people to fill, no more poor attitude
for me, negativity will seize, illness makes my eye's freeze, ignore the
troubled mind of who's sick, be careful of lust because women will tease,
healing the touch from God, the Holy-Sprit in the breeze,

A church circus known to me but still to all is unknown

A vision from a poet named Joe, Church awaiting some religion is
complicating, heart to soul, to open the knocking the door to all hearts, from
a sprain to a rupture if I only slept on the floor, I hope I don't split from the
core, at times back still feels sore, Jesus suffered so much gore! People
dying of hunger including baby African's and the poor,

Power to be, new land once from the sea,
God will unlock the door with his golden key, all criminals will flee,
Together all religions will gather for a feast, a perfect world to see, the
faithful will be at peace,

A church circus to me is known still to all is unknown,

By: Joseph John Thomas
1-25-08

11

"A Lonely Soul"

God goes on an, on an, on,
A deer to raise its first fond,
God is with me a forever a trust bond,
God is with me past , present, and future, forever in history, five
feet beneath, bone's weary, cracking to seep,

Living with God is priceless,

A lonely soul who not fool, through God I'm and everyone can be
his golden soul, a lighting bolt, a young colt,

Plan's waiting, God's Holy-Sprit is penetrating and evil is
vanishing, God is Love even the bible is complicating, forever soul
to soul, heart to heart, love to a gang, the ratio of a big bang could
we began all over, a man's lucky clover,

Volunteering for a group, sipping on some tasty soup,
God's people will reign, live for eternity to keep insane to sane
through blood to vain, God's Holy- Spirit to refrain, to relive
aggravations, Holy- Spirit sensation, a remedy to cure retardation,

Living soul to soul, a lonely soul who not to fool,

                                    By: Joseph John Thomas
                                    1-29-08

"A New World A New Heaven"

A waterfall of purity to a transparent of beauty,
A rainbow to show with the glow of rain and sunlight,
Across every hill and prairie, to believe in God, like Peter Pan to a
fairy, the love of God will carry, Comino a nickname from a rap
song, made music from a bong, trying to write new lyrics to form a
song,

A new world a new heaven the glory of God so precious forever
breathless,

Through delusions that are very complicating, to God to man, to
God I'm his number one fan, God will bring a new world a new
land, No one going hungry it's a free meal! Allowing time to go by
with a blink of an eye, the sun is giving off a glow a paradise God
will show, a sunset will set for you and I,

A new world a new heaven the glory of God so precious forever
breathless,

Hot springs to everyone, kid's having so much fun, A part of the
bible is unknown, a new world unwritten to print, God is waiting a
new world a new heaven that is fitting,

By: Joseph John Thomas
3-4-08

"The Fire"

God the creation the creator, believing Jesus the savor, Life saver,
Healing to and from, in the presents of Jesus, the preacher, a beloved teacher
through the word of God and the faith of his people,

Blue, red, white, yellow green, God's the fire, the chapter, were in the bible,
Take a part, and were in the scene, the creator, could he be cut and lean?,
were a journey to complete our dreams, we belong in a world, together
sewed on the seems, God's chosen us on the journey to follow his path, the
killers will feel his wrath,

Sprits drifted to the light, announcing the coming, it's in sight, lifted hands,
arms and voices, God gives rules of life, it's your right, Christians reaching
for the sky, believe me God doesn't lie, a sign of peace a dove will fly,

The fire trapped in many hearts to you and I, wondering souls in the sky,
remember written commandments in brick or stone, God's with us were not
alone,

The fire, the sun, a building fire like through all nuns,
The believers the receivers, a catcher need to find the reliever, God is trust
worthy to the preachers, to forgive we all sin, only time will tell, a hit of a
church bell,

The fire, running through all veins like an electric wire, feeling the gift from
God, the right mood, like energy from food, God lives through us, baby's
will cry, feeling a great high,

The fire is life through the sun, someday with a great feast, with the light we
will meet, solid ground, cold on my feet, Sprit lifted high through the sky,
forever through to live indeed we all started from a seed!

By: Joseph John Thomas

2-14-08

"The Forbidden Door"

North to west east to south, east to west, a key to open a buried chest, X spotted with gold and gems, Email to send, with the root beer blend,

The forbidden door, secret's to tell, double boiler, sweet corn kettle, a personal care home, for me a place not to settle,

Door one, door two, door three, the white light, the Holy-Sprit to see, all diamonds will flee the devil is on his knee's, for a second chance, rapture to appear, lost souls in search of light,

The forbidden door, God's tears, let it pour, money will flow to the rich not to the poor, the forbidden, the forbidden door, I'm on the count to four, God will forget the pimp's and the whores, An eagle will soar, living souls, will shine, with God in vine, Those seeing, will be heavenly believing, faithful still receiving,

God will open heavenly door and lock and forget the forbidden door,

By: Joseph John Thomas
1-31-08

" A Night Time Story"

When the hours become seconds of a hundred years of life,
A beat of a heart that lasted more than infinity beats,
The love between a man and a women, that begun at their young adult age,
A respect to be granted as the air we breathe to honor our holy father,
The sunlight to give life from a seed, a common wealth to do a special deed,
To the creation of human, a light of God to last from sea to sea,
The old man's last thought, to all of his teachers of knowledge of what has taught,
The elderly man is closing his eye's to reach the sun through clouds of the blue skies,
A good dream one day to become reality, a dense fog to feel lifted like without gravity,
A rainbow to show the purity, of the colors of Mother Nature, The Holiness to create, the kid turning eighteen going on his first date, a trust with God's good graces, to return a smile that brings in many happy faces, To embrace a enjoyable life, God made us equal a life to remain sometimes complex like a movie to await for it's sequel, a soft voice to well known words, to a bow of kneeling head to be knighted from a sword,
A night time story to entertain a young child, To a boy to sleep without being afraid, to faint asleep to fade like a name on the grave, A volunteering award to a signature of a gift card, the love of happiness to God's fulfilled promise,

By: Joseph Thomas
5-29-08

"A Paradise"

God will show to the blind, the devil and the sinners will beg to forgive, to a prayer to everlasting life, a bright light to see, a flare of light to see, a flare of light of a shadow to a blind man will see, Negativity will flee,

A pause of silence to see of one spring day, the work of God, a paradise, remember it took God seven day's, year to year, tear after tear, joy is at a coming of a paradise of an enhanced earth,

A paradise God will show, to the furthest star, to were God's earth core, to famous to the poor, sinners will remorse for mercy, people will walk and sing gospel, to remember a dinosaur from a fossil,

Coping skills not needed because of God's beauty, five senses at a shock of believing, a human being is going to be in paradise of God's magnificent love for you and I, a first born bird will fly,

Time will freeze, God's constant Holy-spirit breaks through the leaves, a paradise God will show to the furthest star to the earth's core,

By: Joseph John Thomas
3-4-08

"A Seed"

To give life from the sun and water,
To sprout from a seed to a flower from the Holy mother and father,
A seed to form into a tree to bloom from a leaf from nutrients five feet beneath,
A tree to grow bigger and stronger, one day to bare fruit to human to prevent hunger,

A golden yellow seed to give life to the earth and to the sun a touch from Holiness a world of completeness,

The brotherly love from family of brothers, the protection of an older brother brought together from a family connection that is stronger, to live forever through the beginning of a seed of God that plants in everyone of us that becomes reborn as a Christian, a smile as contagious that ends up in laughing, that wind's up in being breathless, a seed in the virgin marry of a life of Jesus to be sinless,

A golden yellow seed to give life to the earth and to the sun, a touch from Holiness a world to completeness,

A seed to carry and breed of more creations to fulfill God's sensations, the love to carry to one another to give thanks to the Holy mother and father, for some the work to paint a large painting of the earth to the beginning or to the birth of a seed,

By Joseph John Thomas
4-22-08

"A Storm before Night"

A rain before a long hard work day,
A nap on my bed where I lay,
A storm before night, a lightning bolt that is in sight,
I kneel before God and praise him for the air that I breathe tell I die and be part of God,
To not part to love Jesus through God with all my heart,
The sun that sprouted the seed for this earth to Holiness of a cloud of fog to see hand and
hand to the Holy land, where grass and tree's to be pollinated by bees,
Soon to become fruit to soothe tongue and throat,
To fill hunger with a warm welcome light of God,
To build within to a friend no matter what the color of the human's skin,
To be healed of shark cartilage from human to a sharks skin,
Jesus died for us so we could forgive our sins,
To be a Christian so many hang out on the limb,
To limit the days without sin, through Jesus God will forgive,
To try and live a pure life for the hundred tears that I live!

By: Joseph Thomas
6-6-08

"A Vision"

A vision to care and share to love one another like a couple or a pair,
To only be explained in such exact detail to fill an empty pail.
To love a vision through me to you through love of God to share with many
through me and you, Becoming faint to reality through my illness through
positively, a clue to fin the light to me and you, a gift of God through
delusions one day to be illusions, to a fairy tail to motivate to carry the
empty pail and fill it with a vision to me to you,

A vision so real to be signed and sealed,

Let life carry you with the help of the word of God with a new world yet still
to come and share with everybody will see the beauty, let the love grow like
jack and the bean stock with a seed of glory and Holy,

A picture in the bible of cupids and angels flying high, many rainbows
featuring in the sky with every church embraced with peace among all to
who believes who asks may will receive,

A vision so real to be signed and sealed,

By: Joseph John Thomas
2-5-08

"God goes on and on"

God the creator, a seed to food to enter the mouth,
East to west, north to south, pole to pole, a magnetic force,
Through God he is our only source,

God goes on and on to the break of don,

Boy and girl to a husband to buy his love a white necklace white
pearl,
A seed now a tree, growth from sunshine and water, to build a
building or a road brick by brick, God will find peace in the middle
east, to my visions like a diamond heart, to and from God a
friendship that will never part,

God goes on and on to the break of don,

A present to unwrap, Gods love to fill in the`gap, a sore toe, now
cured by a tree's sap, an old man's dream to escape from a nap,
A watch to tell time, Gods Holy-Spirit to stay inline, my brother to
pay off his speed limit fine, only God can tell, Jesus at all doors to
ring the bell,
Praying, God will heal, time will tell, selling products that won't
sell, organic food is limited, holes to fill in soon, the ship entering
out of the lagoon,

God goes on and to the break of don,

By: Joseph John Thomas
1-25-08

"God is Beautiful"

The caring of a baby to be born, a leaflet or a petal on a rose,
A smell of a fresh scent of a droplet of water to shine or ricochet,
A sight of a beautiful blossomed rose bush, yes indeed and is all
started from a seed,

God is beautiful, like a fruit to be colorful and tasteful,

Oxygen from blue blood now red from a bruise to a cut, mixed
people, a dog to be called a mutt, Energy from food, thanking God
to be in the right mood, pizza, ice cream, remember all natural
made at one time, taking either herbs or medication to stay inline,
God will show in the days of spring a morning bird to sing,

God is beautiful, like a fruit to be colorful and tasteful,

A tree to bare fruit of all to consume as a flower to bloom to a tree
of a fall day to collect sap a taste from a spoon, a new paradise that
is coming soon, A beautiful day all different kinds of birds, to a
Christian to pass the word of God, a sunny day to count on, the
blaze of a sunset, to the melting snow on a spring morning, the
mist on a lake soaked in on the lily pads and the tip of a tree frogs
echo of the bullfrogs croaking,

God is beautiful, like fruit to be colorful and tasteful,

By: Joseph John Thomas

3-4-08

"God is everyone and everything"

To interpret a passage about a Greek God,
To erase the anger by unspoken words through a positive action,
The love of God is hard to figure for some, a man to his brother, a
birth from his mother, God's only son suffered for our sins, a last
weeks tear left over from some sand in the eye from some pus,

God is everyone and everything, in church to worshiping from
gospel to sing, to fly with a broken wing, a piece of bread an
opposite of poison led, every morning to make my bed,

Rapping Christian music, not a fluke, to everyone to suit, to make
a harmony by a flute, a worn out boot, an argument, no need to
bother, a plan to soar over, a hand shake from his brother,

By: Joseph John Thomas
3-8-08

"God is more than great!"

Studying the bible to imitate readings from the father to his
daughter, to a silver crucifixion cross that I where with pride, I was
baptized Catholic, I have nothing to hide, To fill your heart with
the Holy Ghost, we eat the food and wine were the host,
A chip of flint to spark, for the Christians were on a voyage like
Luis and Clark,

God is more than great, put God first in your life with grace to set a
pace,

reduce littering to help save the planet, remember the Indians
didn't waste anything, A gift of God to tell the future, the Love of
God will last forever, a shy dog now alert, a smell of a bone in the
dirt, step after step a stairway to heaven to get there for the
righteous don't need to believe in the lucky number seven,
God is more than great; a flower energized from the sun nectar to
be honey from a bee so tasty to your tongue, a bee is not just a bug,

God is more than n great, put God first in your life with grace, to
set the pace,

You will taste and see, God is powerful remember he separated the
sea, Grandmother's grandchild sleeping, no more tea, all Christians
and Jews appearance or spirit will last, a holy soul from the past, a
new earth at one spring day, a swiping gasp of the Holy Spirit, to
forever will last were on God's list to finish the task,

By: Joseph John Thomas
3-7-08

"God is with us"

Through the sad times,
God is with us,
Through the thick and thin,
 God is with us,
Happiness God laugh's with us,
Swaying leaves back and forth,
God breath's with us,
Soft dripping water on the bead of the ocean, rivers, streams, grass
and terrain,
 God cry's with us,
Through pain and suffering of my back pain or whoever suffers
from back pain,
 God is with you and me,
Grieving over lost ones,
God is with us,

By: Joseph John Thomas
12-31-08

"God's Plan for all"

After a long hard job, to drink an ice cold under an enriched
sassafras tree for shade, a shadow of height to figure, a black ink
football players signature, the odd number to be born with an
illness, but still have all your senses, bad news for a human to be at
shock, to lose your wallet from a pick it poked, the passion of a
dancer or jock, a lost bird to find it's strength to join it's flock, a
grandfathers grandchildren to wind his grandfather's clock,

God's plan for all , a calling for me that is at stall,

A wild horse for the cowboy to tame to figure out the horses name,
the nervous once a beast to be as a gentle giant, to carve a statue
with a special tool, to take your time for a game of pool, smoke
free that's the way to be cool, God's the air, were polluting his
world, he will stay calm to a cat to purr, a hunter to eat meat from
an animal, to respect the animal to an Indian to ware it's fur, no
carrion by the curb, so many options to choose, why be an
alcoholic, why drink booze, a hang over of a deathly snooze,
temptation for the sensation is at a stall for a creation, a Christian,
a rebirth, I'm for the love of God and to live for him is what it's
worth,

God's plan for all, a calling for me that is at a stall,

Occupation or careers brings skills to learn, always money to be
earned, a look on the kid's face to be scorned, one day driving to
work on corn oil, a growth of religion is at a broil, planting crops
from soil, to announce the coming of a feast to whether to find the
right time, for Christians to walk the fine line,

God's plan for all a calling for me that is at a stall,

By: Joseph John Thomas 3-28-08

"God's Rose Bush"

Full of emotion to spread the word of God, to church to church, to
Jehovah witness's knocking door to door on the porch, pass the
love of God like an Olympic torch,

A thorn that lives through all season's, an elderly man lived
through all season's, to find his calling, his life reason, to why he's
on earth, the trait of life, a seed of the creator, a man and woman's
face of tears to a baby's birth, love is priceless not what it's worth,
A girl or a boy, either or to decide it's up to God and the stronger
cell to genetics, a stillborn then family are sympathetic,

God's Rose Bush, red a color of passion to a human of his
creation,

A thorn to grow back on a cows broken horn's, a troubled child to
get scorned, a fortune of Gold to a founder of a lucky man, to give
back to his community, a fortune to keep his sanity through God in
hand and hand, Jesus fasted in the hot beating sand, now to wait
for the summer heat, to bloom of a rose bush, a new paradise, a
new heavenly land, to compete with man, A baby boy or girl to
take his or hers first breathe, years to come from drought to sand
to God's seed to his life long plan,

Room for everyone, not crowded, no more starving people, God to
prepare the temple,

God's rose bush, red a color of love, forever is a passion to a
human is his creation,

By: Joseph John Thomas

3-20-08

"I Love You God"

I love you God from the power of my heart to the depths of the sea,
The brain that God created,
The special time for God of white lights to be concentrated,
Special touch as meat to be marinated,
The blue blood in my veins enriches like food to cranes,
 I love you God now and infinity,
 Through times of sanity,
 The time of crisis in temptation,
As God's there in the moment for creation,
Through the power of the mind,
To the clues of a paradise to hold onto like a metal vise,

By: Joseph Thomas

"The Formula"

As I write these words to a scientific formula,
For God to create the paradise,
To have words that has so much meaning and remember God has no price,
A life to be complete,
God will provide more as he will create,
No more worries of elderly with their fate,
When God finds the formula just as this earth,
Like oxygen to fill to flow across, back and forth,
A paradise that the Holy light and Jesus will bring,
An Island inside an Island that contains walls of waterfalls, fruit trees and fruit cactus,
that is still unknown, but a seed that God will create,
Like women and man the joy to mate,
The relationship that I have with God,
As close as soul in the fog,
All four leaf clovers in the grass, Rich soil to bring life to any seed,
As fresh protein inside the fruit cactus rich fat to heat the entire cactus is edible and
useful,
 The end for money to pay the toll,
The time of God to create the paradise as careful to a game of poll,
Through the love of God and prayer and new words of God to share,
Through the stars that might seem so close,
But a cloud of dust and light to the night time sky will glair,
As the light will glow with flair,
The new Atmosphere to every color blue to the sky,
The power of Gods formula will fill the earth to helium to a balloon,
A new life with the combination of my mind to Gods Holy creation,
To his humans sensations,

By: Joseph John Thomas
10-5-08

"A Holy Seed"

A great distance across the earth rotating around the sun a holy seed is being prepared,
the Holiness of God and the Goddess to bring life to the Holy seed,
To humans which are loved and cared,
 One spring day to pray for a Holy seed to sprout,
In the darkness of space and the shining sun,
To give honor to the father and the son,
 to curl your fingers as you do and lay them down as a large mountain to hold two
waterfalls on each side and to flow to springs of the earth heated the water to layers of
warmth of comfort to bathe,
To God's imagination to a paradise that will be made in the mater of time,
The largest four mountains baring the eight waterfalls with four rainbow's in the mist,
A sign in the sky to our earth as visible at night,
 In the space with a light of God's grace,
Just for human's and made for the followers of the faithful and believers of God to get
there as easily as fish in a pod, The mountain made inside with gold on the outside and
the inside made with granite and iron,
 A life of purity and a perfect paradise for humans,
 A fruit cactus already there in the grass and terrain a root of nutrients that will bare fruit
of vitamins and minerals and the cactus will be made up of protein and all nutrients there
will be seeds to create more, at least a thousand at each side of the waterfalls,
A paradise to come from the light of the Holy sun, Oh boy with a paradise day of fun,
Nudity as common of a nudity beach, A pure and habitable for all ,
The greatest making of God to Mankind to a new moon A new earth,
A Holy seed from birth of a God and Goddess of purity to finesse, A Holy seed to bring
the mother load of one spring day of a perfect life,

By: Joseph John Thomas
6-26-08

" A One Spring Day"

There lay in the soil a seed, which is three inches in the ground,
A raindrop to give the seed a root to bare life of a leaflet,
In the dark a hanging leaflet shivers by the nighttime air,
 A one-spring day to bare fruit and the legacy of the future orchard known to mankind,
As well known to a seed and a Holy- Spirit to first birth from the sun,
One buried seed in the ground for the winter and decomposed leaves for the growth of a one spring day,
A one-spring day is yet to arrive,
The smell of prairie grass to awake the den of the lion's pride,
To a gust in the air to carry to the front of a beach tide,
No need for anger against God he's always on our side,
A one-spring day is yet to arrive,
As the mans imagination grew bigger as the mans relationship grew stronger,
The day awaits a paradise, I wonder how much longer,
A Holy seed as the earth is here for proof,
Shows that God bares seeds to sprout life of humans to fruit,
No need for meats from animal's protein from inside of a fruit cactus,
Natural fresh water glaciers to provide water for the waterfalls,
Rivers flowing of paved gold on the bottom of the river floors,
Holy-Spirits with the joining of light a paradise with one-spring day humans will take flight,

By: Joseph John Thomas
9-17-08

God's the Gentle Voice

Self-conscious brings through a thought,
Ten Commandments was the fire bush with what God has taught,
A whisper of two hungry mice, a pause to look for a couple or a
spouse, a snap there goes the mouse a cat on the pounce,
A boy learning manners to prayer's a Christian looking through the
bible with an emotion of a deep stare, the fire flair, and One day
the boy is going to be like his grandfather and grandmother the true
pair,

A gentle voice is God through a peaceful returning prayer,

A chess battle to a sloppy baffle, laughing is a gift from God to
win the game of chess or is at a stalemate, living day to night, God
will find you in the search of light,

A gentle voice is God through a peaceful returning prayer,

An old man's dried up tear, through an artist's deep stair, to a
couple or a broken up pair, A fire to burn to keep warm from a
kettle and some woodchips, a baby to be born, a teenager hooked
on porn, to live without drugs, to have a cute pug,

God's the gentle voice through a peaceful returning prayer,

By: Joseph John Thomas
2-1-08

"Healing in the Cold"
Living trying not to sin, let God forgive, forgiving still living,
Love not hate, I'm a Christian everyday, God never betrays.
Loving for everything that he has shown,
A call on a ring tone, calling for Jesus love through him peace
needs us, a wound to heal, through skin, no pus, a girl without lust,
No need for a criminal, God will find just,

Healing in the cold, still strong and bold,

A man, only in mind, every day with a pill,
A promise to fulfill, so much has passed, a sick man with his last
gasp, Tuff legs remember Jesus had to fast, an hour glass to freeze,
memories from the past,

Healing in the cold, still strong and bold,

Life is like a game,
Lifting weights to get lean,
Remember were Christians were on the same team,
Icy Hot to relieve pain, talking to God outside to keep sane,
A touch me not to pop. To fulfill God's theory or plot,
Live for what we have got.

Healing in the cold, sill strong and bold,

By: Joseph John Thomas
1-29-08

"I'm still alive"
Back attach, Doctor's think I'm whack,
Bear pinned the lead wolf, just for food,
Bipolar makes me feel that high and low mood,

I'm still alive, just feeling the music for a vibe,

Blue denim jeans, a friend to only part to a crack fiend,
The actor preparing for the drama scene,
I like cinnamon my chest look feminine,
All natural high, a cloud of Jesus in the sky,
A fish eating his pray, easy to find with a hunter to its beagle,

Still alive feeling the music for a vibe,

I'm still alive, for those green leaves and chives, don't worry
because I'm on your side, Believe me because I don't lie, really,
Trying to not act so silly like a crowded place like Philly,
Pennsylvania's winters can be chilly,

I'm still alive feeling the music for a vibe,

By: Joseph John Thomas
1-31-08

Is this the right time?

Every day taking medication from a pill bottle,
An illness to set me away from a racing thought,
To a word to rime with poetry,

Is this the right time?

To obey or stay inline of the rules in the good book or bible,
To manage the pressure of a rapid storm of waves to form, A hurricane to
form as the blood flow just in my brain, yet I'm still sane, to be free of
toxins, to filter water, to be nourished from a mother to an infant from a
baby's cry, to a nursery rime,

Is this the right time?

A goal to trigger a dream, another draft pick to continue to form a football
team, oxygen for an old widow, to finish the rip or tear on the seam of a
worn out pair of jeans,

Brick by brick to build a castle for a king, rappers earning for a bling, bling,
a necklace made from pearls that is remained in the Queen's jewelry box, a
red fox in the den, a new generation of cat's, to find a name tag for one,
picking up a stray cat, a young girl's eye's open as wide as a game of chess,

Is this the right time?

When the chaos became written of the golden ink, of the brittle scroll, with a
ribbon to be sealed, a century later to form the dollar bill, and a prophesies to
fulfill, now inquired by law to follow the old man's Patten, a world ahead so
make sure your seatbelt is fastened,

Is this the right time?

So set assail unless you're stuck in jail, and let your dreams come true!

By: Joseph John Thomas
2-24-08

"Joe's quotes and short poems"

" Positively is contagious, it's like a disease or a virus, you'll be more happy around someone that is positive"

" God is life and he will provide you and I with sanity and happiness, the strength within yourself and through God will help make positive changes in your life"

Find the power deep inside yourself to overcome the evil, anger, and self-pity, that has or was been building inside someone,

"Time"

Time is patience,
Time sometimes seems forever to wait,
Time might take time to settle,
Time will tick tock,
Time is forever precious,
But time will tell when the time is right,

" The Lonely Bear"

The lonely bear could not shed a tear,
The lonely bear had pain, pain within fear,
But the lonely bear could not shed a tear,
Thoughts of the bear to scare the frightful deer,
But still the bear could not shed a tear,

"Peace"

Will the world ever be in peace?
For some, will the world continue to spread the word of God?
God is peace with the power within to calm the human with the peaceful wind, God is love now and to the beginning of time,
God in the making, Angels will sing,
God is happy, when his people will rejoice,

By: Joseph John Thomas
7-14-07

36

"The Mysterious White Fog"

Grandma always told me, crack a white rock to find your
initials,
A pupil to become a renewed soul, following a path of
purity, now a crystal bed of diamonds to form a waterfall,

The white mysterious fog, by the feet of Adam and Eve, for
God to bring life, a fog to bring a new heaven and earth, no
money or greed, a perfect world for God to sew the seed, to
Jesus died for us, knocking on the door of unbelievers and
unfaithful, a warmth that God will bring, a choirs will sing,

Memories lost of grown-ups, but once were baby's, God
remembers every thing, the love to a lost love hug, A
awkward sound from an open forest of frogs, crickets, each
one of us has the world in our hands, God gave us the
golden ticket, a crackling voice of an old man suffering
from a disease, a shot of insulin, so kind to say please and
thank you, a mourning awakening sound of a beautiful
woman's voice singing with the flock of birds, God made
us, a criminal finding just, mankind help make this earth
what it is, pollution limiting air, were hindering God's flair,
God loves us and he will always care,

By: Joseph John Thomas
3-11-08

"The Pink Light"

A baby born in the womb, a loud cry of an infant almost to be
born, his or her mother's caring loving hands,
The pink light reflecting off the baby's eye's from his or her
mother's womb, a baby to be born very soon,
A nine month pregnant women once as big as a balloon,

A loud piercing cry, and out came a one of a kind Christmas eve
baby boy, a rapping present of joy came to his mother and father,
One left foot and one right foot sunk in the plaster engraved his
name Joseph John Thomas,

Terrible two's was a battle to stay focused on what to be tolled, so
much has passed as a young toddler, I still sometimes put my right
foot in my left shoe, my name is Joe and as a child now a grown-
up, my favorite color is still blue,

Being born through the pink light, now looking in the sun to filter
in the vitamin k, the lost puppy loves to play, may I or please, a
wild hoarse to a cowboy to say at ease,

A name that came from my parents to change is up to you, as you
get older as time passes, men and women get bolder, a romantic
song your mate to hold her, global warming may be at time colder,
summertime melting of the icecaps a warm up after walking laps, a
tea like yerba to burn of fat, a memory of a swooping bat in my
hair a child, losing weight, remember I was fat!

The pink light as a newborn hungry for milk, now a grown up,
designing on paper one day to silk,

By: Joseph John Thomas
3-13-08

"The white light, Shines"
God's the light no need to be afraid,
In the bible God's in every page,
An Indian to find the herbal sage,
White men found the way by a compass or gage,

The white light shines, the white light shines, the earth to reveal
signs,

Buried behind the color of the eye, the white light shines,
To a person that is even blind, touch to feel, God is everything that
is real, God's the white behind the color of the eye, mama's first
child to say goodbye,

God will fight, his glory and his might, the white light is in sight,
Though tears and blood to rain to pour, tell the sun to the earth
core, From scratch, God made us from cell to atom to DNA, I've
always prayed connecting to every bone, were not alone, a painted
statue in stone,

The white light shines, the white light shines, the earth to reveal
signs,

By: Joseph John Thomas
1-28-08

"The White Moving cloud"

In the air lies a cloud, moving through a mountain,
So high an airplane could be fooled,
The white cloud holding in moisture, now gray and a moist drift in the air,
A rain cloud, letting teardrop of water pressure,
A rainbow to feature, all eyes are at a stare, like all different nutrients and
flavors of all fruits, for a human being to suit,

The white moving cloud, looking for the right shape to fit your mood,

The sun is shining through all clouds are visualized by a stream of an
lightened highway to heaven, different clouds, sizes, shapes, and forms of
clouds to be reached by a bird , a touch to feel a gift from a notebook in a
recipe, flavor from a cook,

The white moving cloud, looking for the right shape to fit your mood,

A smile of a dimple, Who made the earth? Was it so simple? Drips from
rain, a flower pulled from soil, to grow from ground to soil, to sprout
different colors, of every flower pollinated from a bee, energy from honey,
to mix with other foods,

The white moving cloud, looking for the right shape to fit your mood,

Floating high in the sky a cloud awaits, the sun light an object appears
insight, fog on earth an object so blurry, a rabbit to scurry, a seed to bury,
racing time for crops, I'm in such a hurry, A white moving cloud froze in the
shape of a face, an old man's smile or a frown, or a puzzled look, to find
what might be the cause even to sprit to mind, to find the mystery of love, a
kiss to remember, a baby to an adult, a friendship with God that will never
part,

The white moving cloud looking up, just a right a shape to fit your mood,

By: Joseph John Thomas
2-15-08

"The White Tornado"

A bright light across the horizon,
God's stars on a journey around the earth's hemisphere,
A white tunnel across the moonlight reflecting of the galaxy,
The moon with the shape of a face of a smile of happiness,
enlightened the nighttime sky, the Holy-Spirit is featured with a
gasp of wind to blow away sin,

A white tornado is sideways with the clouds forming a breeze,
catching and evaporating the smoke of an old mans cigarette as he
sneezed,

A white tornado to blow away, please God, stay!

On my knee's I pray, to vanish hunger from African's
A delusion, now to become real, a fruit cactus to appear, love of
God, I'm so sincere, one day it will appear,

A white tornado to blow away, please God, stay!

By: Joseph John Thomas
2-11-08

Who Made God?

No beginning, no end,
A life of eternity, after the world of beauty,
To gather of thoughts, to continue a mind of sanity,
The Alpha and the Omega, the father and the mother, a creator to
give words to a preacher, the mother for the omega a flower to be
born from nature,

The galaxy of stars to the little dipper, to soothe the wind from the
fiddle on the roof to nutrients from a root,

The God's of heaven to form stars, to a fog across the sky, stars
hard to appear from carbon monoxide, the connection of stars to
form Greek mythology to form of history, Who made God?, to
many powerful god's to be proven by stars, there always will be a
God to see science of astronomy, a warmth of God everyday to be
sunny,

The North Star to be guided to stare at the sun to be blinded, An
explosion of life to create a new star, look we and God has came so
far, a picture on the wall, of remembrance of a love one, the creator
to give life from the sun,

The God's of heaven to form of stars, a connection to form God's
of all,

Believing in one truly ultimate being, an open world of seeing, The
sun of life giving life to form a life to a seed to a root to a sperm
and a egg to form a human being,

By: Joseph John Thomas
3-25-08

Why Me?

An illness to be near or close as a sickness,
Why me?
To be born with an illness, not to be known until a teenager to have more
adrenalin then a winning football game,
To be granted three wishes and to be granted one without an illness,
The mania of an illness to God to his creations,
Why me?
To be born with a chemically imbalanced brain, to try to slow down
thoughts like a rush through traffic, to God he is a great dynamic,
Love is expressed in ways of trust with God the father, to be loved by
another the brotherly love of my brother, a great swirl of wind to awake the
homeless man with an illness,
Why me?
To ware the cotton to the cloth of wool of a sheep, to keep warm to the
gathering of bees to part from a swarm,
To put ideas from pen and paper, to house rules to follow, to awake from a
chirping swallow,
Laughing to me is also healing, to a touch can be a warm feeling, an elderly
man's slow processed thought is the wisdom to know of a bed time story, an
action or a feeling to express, to a strategy, like a game of chess,
Being thankful for the now and here, being healthy in the body and mind,
together through family and friends of all different kinds,

By: Joseph John Thomas
5-14-08

"Before Time"

When there is just one God and no earth just sun and light,
God made a join of Holy light,
To see the image of creation through God's sight,
The white light of God to imitate human of man to women,
Before time and when God the land within seven blessed days,
To human to burnt skin of sun rays,
God made a Goddess to join the Holy white light,
To make a human a man and a women,
People Know God as one,
As true as both white lights to match the sky blue,
To love of the highest of all who believed in Jesus,
Before time were the God and Goddess,
Together made every bird,
To a prophet true to his word,
Through God's mouth through thought,
A peaceful dinner through a prayer of thanks for food
A seed to a plant to match God's mood,
The ultimate power of two,
The Holy lights or God and Goddess created for me and you,

By: Joseph John Thomas
9-20-08

"Soul by Soul"

A death in the family,
Grieving to keep sanity,
A closed coffin bought from charity,
A breeze to comfort a cold soul, the sound of chirping crickets,
A crouching rabbit hiding in the thickets,
Lifelong memories, to campfire stories,
Soul by soul to carry by heat of wind, to not hinder without sin,
The love of the Holy-Sprit will comfort your soul as souls pass,
A lost one to carry the joys from the past,
Life may seem difficult to stay true to yourself as the flavor as salt,
Energized to enjoy life like a young colt,
To cuddle at night or sleep alone,
 to communicate to a love one by telephone,
A nighttime star why does it seem so far,
To twinkle and glow to the nighttime sky,
As the comfort of God, with soul by soul,
I will never die,

By: Joseph John Thomas
9-24-08

The Chemically Imbalanced Brain

The slow stuttered slur of a mentally ill child to a fast talked erupt speech from a toddler, to a well known fiddler, a loud obscured sound from the ajar weary of the door of the weary house, lived there was an elderly man that just lost his spouse the noise became as silent as a dream from a mouse, the morning awoke from the ring of a alarm clock with a swat of the fathers flick of a wrist, Doctors evaluated the grandchild of the elderly man, two different times with a pause of silence of two words came out of the psychiatrists mouth By-polar and Schitsophactive, a boy that was emotionally saddened of his fathers dropped chin and tear filled eye's as like a storm of a swaying weeping willow tree of droplets running off the leaves, the fathers flashback of his child being hyperactive and seeing shadows, the room fell quiet with a stare at the psychiatrist, as the father looked at the doctor with a deep stare like a owl to it's pray, and the fathers deep thoughts like as a cloud filled with moisture and dust my fathers ponder look and the doctor suggested many medications but for him only one in mind, a look of love from father to son, as they walked out in the breeze was a blow of fall leaves seemed as a whistle from Gods mouth a warming chill in the air, as the boy went to bed he prayed as a cold night with the boy's willpower and strength, through God in faith,

By: Joseph Thomas
6-3-08

"The Imagination of a Child"

The silence of a child is golden, the imagination of a child is priceless,
To imaginary friends, to the worry of parents of the child talking to himself,
like a whisper of leaves rattling, the boy impresses his talents to one day
maybe be an actor, to keep him quiet give him a piece of now and later, that
is a piece of candy, to help with chores the boy comes in handy, an unsolved
mystery with a piece of candy on the floor, A boy's nightmare to remember
an unwanted memory an image to a fright maybe a memory of the rest of his
life, A monster under your bead, just a joke to scare, though parents will
always care, a loving mother and father either or maybe just one, the
warming of the sun, feeling the love of God is helpful to all, to some even a
calling to the places in need, a glow of a holy seed, to the boy's happy
dream, to the comfort of his parents to the remembrance of who suffered on
the cross, as easy as a child to understand to follow the Christian faith like
Jesus' footprints in the sand, to when he returns the imagination of a
paradise and a new land, A holy earth but for how long, through the
harmony of a song, the imagination of God to a child as like a cloud opening
up one day to the gift of God through a dream to a prayer as we all prayed,

By: Joseph Thomas
6-4-08

"The Last Star"

When time freezes and the earth slows to its last rotation,
A human with his eye's open with tears of joy,
Knowing that something beyond words that can be explained,
To tell from day to night,
But with a star to show us and guide us to the light of heaven,
To years of science theory's to tell the end of time,
To a new earth, but how many years to bring life of the last star,
Through God's life to a human being,
To cut down a tree to limit breathing,
The God that started all,
A meteorite to end it all,
A Holy seed to bear a fruit of the earth,
To a baby's eyes open at birth,
A life century, as much has passed for an old man to see the last star,
 The sun will last thousands of years,
God's creation still in progress,
Of the star that gave life from the Holy God and Goddess,

By: Joseph Thomas
6-14-08

"The Race to the True Paradise"

So many people waits for the return of Jesus what day how long same church same hymn song, all come together to live on a True Paradise, souls, spirits with God and Jesus, No evil spirits the trinity will be strong like always when people search and find through all human race to meet God's love through his Holy son Jesus like when our heart beats at a pace, This earth and the true paradise filled with the Holy-Spirit and our Lord Savior Jesus Christ, A physical place of the return of Jesus that is plentiful, Double size the earth and you the True paradise at view from the earth, made from the imagination of me the power of the white light of God and Jesus, peace will find us, No more salt water or sea, A coming spring day will stop you in your tracks, but those will know it is the return of Jesus, Just like how the bible teaches us, were on the race to the paradise so if your not waiting, no contemplating just open the door and the power of our Lord will give you enough, rich or poor everybody's welcomed to the race to the paradise so stretch your arms and legs a run to a True paradise of Fruitful fun into the hands of our Holy-Spirit witch is our creator a face in the eye's of God and Jesus our savior,

By: Joseph John Thomas
Visionary and Prophet of God and Jesus

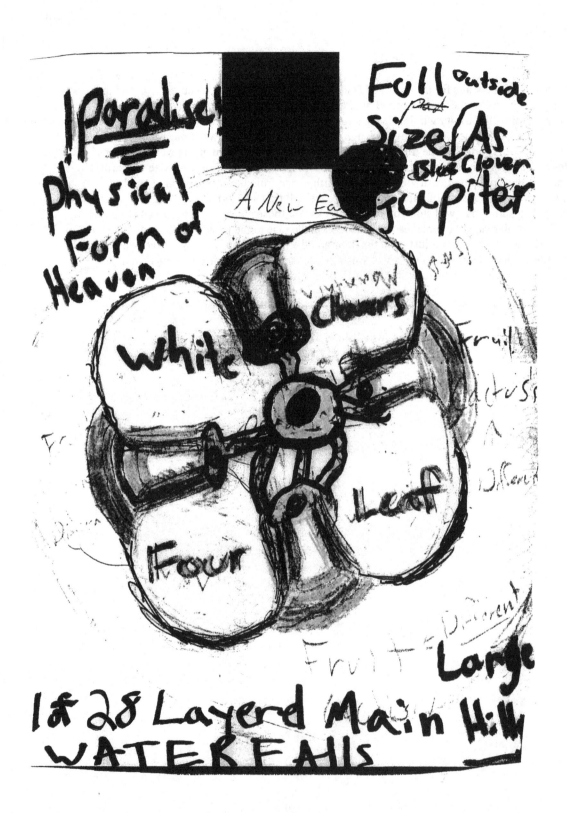

Fruit cactus

RAINBOW
Fruit Cactus

" The Pulse"

The beat, the eye's,
God's piercing eye's,
All blue in the skies,
Flesh and blood,
The pulse that created all,
A visionary on the call,
That the spirit and soul,
with the combination to bring life the power the white light.
the spirit the soul with both,
 anything is created form the Holy-Spirit,
Why question to believe all that is true,
a high power that is within you,

"The Secrets of God"

An explanation through all my poetry,
To a buffoon that is tied up with bottled up anger,
To act on it why not bother,
Find a passion and hold on and never let go,
I write and grow in God,
The secrets of God to tame a gentle giant,
The wind at a ponder as further to land to see and yonder,
From the Godly word pored from my heart to pen and paper,
The sun can be blinded for a few second,
But the eye's of god that is brought to all life,
God will lead you in the right path
As his light keeps you alert of the dare barriers,
Of the dark holes that might be in this earth that we call life,

By: Joseph John Thomas
10-3-08

"The Unknown"

The trust and love of a mysterious object that can be seen through light,
 The power of thoughts can wipe away sins,
The crowded church became silent as the preacher shared the power of God,
 With a swipe of his hand and from mouth a word to cleanse,
 With hands high the righteous people fell with grace back in their chairs,
  That is the feeling of the Holy-Ghost and through the television the power from
Coast to coast,

To know the strength of all the saviors and to remember the date like a reborn
 As a Christian to the unknown powers deep within a preacher,
  To known words studied and taught with great passion,
Missing out for the ones that don't believe, on the edge to stay catholic for
communion that I once received, to everyday to say a prayer before a meal,
 It's unknown to a non Christian to worship God to God's imagination that to a
 cartoonist is to be animated,

The stress of an old man's worries to the unknown combination for a disease or
an illness to be carried, The life long dream to follow the steps of Jesus and to
build your relationship with God,

By: Joseph John Thomas
9-3-08

"Why do I write about God?"

Every word with so much meaning,
A gift from God to express from poetry,
To the last breathe of a solder that is wounded and bleeding,
Every word put together, to kill an insect why not bother,
The odds to be raised without a father,
 God will always be there for me and you,
The life of the sun and sky blue,
I write about God because I love God and what he has provided us,
So much love to his beings,
To the moon, sun, and stars for God to watch over,
Through God birds chirp of Joy as surprised as a kid to unwrap a toy,
The wonder of God to be born as a girl or a boy,
Every leave for energy for us to breathe,
For God to breathe the life of trees to bloom with the showing of a red moon,
To live in the moment to realize and worship on the Holy Sabbath day,
To beasts to beings we where made the love of God will never fade,

By: Joseph Thomas
6-14-08

"Winter Times"

When the wind is at a chill, and I take the prescription pill,
The wind blows the shingle if the old weary house, and the penguin buries
it's head in his shoulders, The ice freezes the water that hits the boulders,
Time is at a stop when the ice cold wind seeps through the cracks of the
century old house, the kids play rattles the old feeble grandfathers clock, the
elderly man having a struggle to put on his holy sock,

Winter times and sun shining mornings of the sun reflecting, awoke the
snoring elderly man,

The bare trees rattle back and forth with the snap of an old stem,
The seeds and roots in the ground suck up the nutrients of one spring day,
Snuggled up tight as the kids prepare to play in the snow, on their way out
there minds our full of life with there smart behaviors of different kinds,
happy as the kids are a cloudy night with no stars

Winter times an sun shining morning of the sun reflecting, awoke up the
snoring elderly man,

By: Joseph John Thomas
1-20-08

Man vs. God

To a building as strong as a tree, a helicopter to design from a bumble bee or a dragonfly, to a vivid airplane in the sky, the slow flying pace of a butterfly to land on a flower to the highest forest to the tallest tower, the peace of the unity of a family, to enjoy a piece of candy, the sound of the ocean in a seashell, a ring of the liberty bell, the mathematic error to the comfort of a animals fur, an impulsive illness to mother nature of a tornado in the distance, a seed to give life from the sun, the luck to make a hole in one, both Man and God work but always have time for fun, the crazy life of a sinner, the luck to be a lottery winner, a killer shark in the ocean, a world of chemicals, I wonder what is Gods potion, the sun to get blisters to relive from some lotion, a movie to see the wonders of a honey bee, God made life of a human, a robot to take simple command to get cold off from the breeze or a paper made fan, a swiping sound, the colors of a rainbow, to measure an illness from the highs and lows God's secret to create a human from head to toe, the love Man vs. God will always show,

By: Joseph Thomas
6-2-08

"I Love You God"

I love you God from the power of my heart to the depths of the sea,
The brain that God created,
The special time for God of white lights to be concentrated,
Special touch as meat to be marinated,
The blue blood in my veins enriches like food to cranes,
 I love you God now and infinity,
 Through times of sanity,
 The time of crisis in temptation,
As God's there in the moment for creation,
Through the power of the mind,
To the clues of a paradise to hold onto like a metal vise,

By: Joseph Thomas

" Fire Flair"

A glow to capture the inside of the eye,
To pick of all humans organize a Holy plan,
God and Jesus at the cross here I stand,

The Fire Flair inside do reason to hide

Darkness will cast shadows,
only to sleep with,
Light to walk the steps of Jesus,
secrets to announce over many
logic explanations,
unraveled to see with all senses,

The Fire Flair thats inside no reason to hide,

Time and patience to calm his people,
 as all to stand at the cross so New Jerusalem,
can be Gods holy temple,
Be pure the will dim,
Jesus will Knock so let him in,
Begone, Begone, Sin!

The Fire Flair that's inside no reason to hide,

White Ball of Smoke

Being born is love,
God's birth is within a second,
electricity friction and great amount of shock waves,
deep within space,
to create a pearly white eye's face,
the beginning of grace,
At now God's birth,
A white ball of smoke,
to the devil to choke,
the first creations,
God and his brother the devil
what a battle and so powerful,

God and I

A coming event only to share with you,
So brilliant of imagination but with God and to soothe,
accumulated all brightness a change of sunlight,
So much beauty no reason to fright,

To you from God and I,

Prophecies and visions to carry like a dove,
a place of heavenly grace,
a Holy destination for excelled creations,
my mind to confuse Einsteins
let world be filled with signs

To you from God and I,

A sailing ship to move through the current
as God's steadiness to a wonderful intimate relationship,
A picture hidden in a picture book,
memorize to come alive,
A cracked window,
of hearing sense of a supernatural power,
echoing of all skies
white lights every ware flying you high,
Heaven here we come,
days of work and exspecially popes, priests, bishops and nuns,

To you from God and I

Signs

Signs are warnings,
return of Jesus will be rewarding,
God gives me visions open your eye's
The changing of the coming skies,
Different butterfly's Turquoise, teal, neon green,
God and Jesus team,
once buterflyise to illumating tiny suns, more light as not heat
Reddish purple florescent pink,
No skunk smell stink,
the 4th 8th 16th 24th mountain layered waterfalls,
each of them God will put an oder to feel,
visions to reveal,
now opened seals

"Manifestation"

could you imagine every little bit of Gold,
 wired to make a human to an angel in Gods mold,
Built to fly with God in the sky,
As human technology is arranged,
to the secrets of God,

A Holy Spirit manifestation is a change on God knows aware when

Angels send messages from God,
But power and love include life,
as God will include his Will,

Different suns, butterfly's are two of my prophecy's
that will happen as the time is Gods satisfaction,
colors in the sky to equal to a crain box,

Extraw

the tribe of Joseph which I include
visions to a seven years
of transporting humans in the whom of God
transforming into a fairy angel and physical form angels
remember this is the manifestation of God,

Diamonds are elegant,
as my words to the eyes of God,
the strength of a gentle giant
through words that only strengthens as God notices,
A New Jerusalem mountain layered waterfalls built up high,
as God' new angels will fly,

 Handy size picking fruit Cactus's'
no harm of all blending flavors with liquid juice inside,
fruit on inside
hills of bouncy cotton fields
fresh star dolphins on the rainbow sand lakes
large flower fairy world,
Singing orchard,
fruity fruit cactus,
spicy vegy cactus,
herb meat vegy cactus,

Island inside an Island

Structure through hundreds of mountain layered waterfalls,
layered for all needs,
living for Goldy giving,
Rainbow of all tones,
waterfalls flowing soft,
water polls to lather,
living in a bedding lining cotton cave inside the 16th layered water fall
ultimate loving touch of God on the Island inside an Island

Conclusion

Your special life purpose:

Your talent is what your good at My life purpose is special
others are different, to work for God is at peace,
your special life purpose is what God Judges you as a person